Easy-to-Make
DOLLHOUSE QUILTS

Janet Armstrong Wickell
Illustrations by the Author

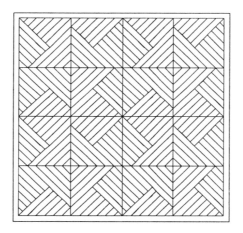

DOVER PUBLICATIONS, INC.
Mineola, New York

Dedication

This book is dedicated to all of the miniature quilt enthusiasts who have attended Minifest. Their love of quilting brings them to the North Carolina mountains in every type of spring weather, from blizzards to rain to wonderful sunshine. Their enthusiasm is contagious.

Other Books by The Author

Quick Little Quilts. The Quilt Digest Press, Lincolnwood, Illinois, 1998. Coauthor, Donna Stidman.

Bibliographical Note

Easy-to-Make Dollhouse Quilts is a new work, first published by Dover Publications, Inc., in 1999.

Library of Congress Cataloging-in-Publication Data

Wickell, Janet.
    Easy-to-make dollhouse quilts / Janet Armstrong Wickell ; illustrations by the author.
        p.   cm.
    Includes index.
    ISBN 0-486-40291-6 (pbk.)
    1. Patchwork—Patterns. 2. Miniature quilts. 3. Doll quilts. I. Title.
TT835.W522   1999
746.46'041—dc21   98-48675
                                                      CIP

Manufactured in the United States of America
Dover Publications, Inc., 31 East 2nd Street, Mineola, N.Y. 11501

Table of Contents

An Introduction to Dollhouse Miniatures

A miniature is usually defined as any reduced-scale version of a larger object. In the world of quilting, show rules often state that miniature entries must be a maximum of 24 inches square, with blocks no larger than 4 inches on a side.

Dollhouse miniatures are made following more specific guidelines. Although dollhouses are available in several scales, the 1:12 scale is the most popular, and is the scale used in this book. The designation simply means that a 12-inch area of the original object is reduced to a 1-inch area in the miniature version. In other words, a 12-inch square block is reduced to a 1-inch square.

Working with such small pieces might at first seem impossible, but don't let the tiny sizes discourage you from making these quilts. All blocks are foundation pieced, which means you do *not* cut and sew together precisely-sized bits of fabric. With this method, even beginners can sew perfect blocks for their dollhouse.

Before you make a quilt, be sure to read the information in the *Dollhouse Quilt Basics* section, beginning on Page 5. It's a good idea to read through all the patterns, too. Foundation piecing is basically the same for every block you'll make, but aspects of one pattern might help you assemble or make design changes to another.

Use the *Quilter's Coloring Book*, beginning on Page 45, to help you determine color value placement. Photocopy the pages, then fill-in the spaces with regular or colored pencils.

I hope you enjoy making these little quilts. And once your dollhouse is furnished, try using the blocks as embellishments for clothing, or as pieced sashing and borders for larger miniature quilts and wallhangings.

—Janet Armstrong Wickell

Getting Started with Fabrics

Selecting Fabrics and Thread

- I recommend you use 100% cotton fabrics for your dollhouse quilts, rather than cotton/polyester blends. Cotton wears well, is easy to work with, and frays less than blended fabrics.
- Match thread content with fabric content. Over time, thread that is stronger than fabric cuts into fibers, creating rips at seams. One hundred percent cotton thread is the best partner for cotton fabrics.
- Other fabric choices include lightweight satins and silks. Note the manufacturer's care instructions when using special fabrics.

Test for Colorfastness

Some dark cottons *bleed*—or lose their dyes, particularly dark purples, blues, and reds. Always test suspected fabrics to be sure they are colorfast.

- Submerge a small piece of fabric in warm, soapy water. See if dye bleeds into water. Or, place the wet patch on a white paper towel. Check to see if dye bleeds onto the towel.

If a fabric bleeds, wash it a few times and check again. If the problem continues, don't use the fabric in a quilt. You might try setting the dye with a commercial fixative, such as Retayne®.

Fabric Shrinkage & Pre-washing

All 100% cottons shrink. Fabrics with low thread counts shrink more than tightly-woven fabrics do, because as fibers relax in water they tend to fill-in the larger gaps between threads. If the blocks in your quilt contain unwashed fabrics that shrink at different rates, distortions will occur when the quilts are dampened. Even small distortions are noticeable in these little quilts, so play it safe and prewash unless you are sure the quilt will never get wet.

Prewashing removes most of the loose sizings and protectants that were applied to fabric at the mill. Use spray starch if you prefer to work with crisper fabrics.

Prewash your fabrics in cool water with a mild, phosphate-free soap.

Understanding Fabric Grain

Have you been to a craft fair, where you watched someone weaving on a loom? Quilting cottons are made in the same way, although much of the process is automated, and on a larger scale.

Long threads, called *warp* threads, are stretched on the loom and secured. These threads become the lengthwise grain of the fabric.

Weft threads are woven back and forth along the entire length of the warp threads. The weft threads become the fabric's crosswise grain.

Selvages, the bound edges along the sides of fabric, are formed when the weft threads change direction as the weaving process travels down the length of the loom.

True *bias* is defined as a 45° angle to the straight of grain, but we refer to any off-grain cut as a bias cut. Fabric is very stretchy along the bias.

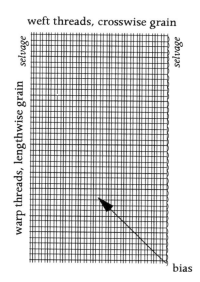

The lengthwise and crosswise threads are both referred to as straight-of-grain, however, the lengthwise grain is less stretchy. Unlike the moving weft threads, warp threads were firmly attached to the loom during the weaving process, and the interlaced weft threads actually help stabilize them. There are usually more warp threads than weft threads per square inch, another stabilizing factor. Lengthwise grain strips make sturdy anchors for quilt borders and sashing.

The following test helps you see the variations in stretch along the different grains

1. Cut a 3-inch square of fabric with edges parallel to the straight grains. Tug on it along the lengthwise grain, then along the crosswise grain. Did you notice a difference in stretch?

2. Now tug on it from corner to corner, along the bias. The fabric will stretch even more, and may become permanently distorted.

Recognizing the different properties of grains gives you a better understanding of why pattern pieces are cut in specific ways.

Selecting Prints

One of the most important aspects of fabric selection is variety. Do you want to make a *scrappy quilt*, one that contains a wide variety of fabrics? Or do you want to follow a more structured, repeating color scheme? Even quilts made with a minimum number of fabrics benefit when you include a variety of print sizes, because they add visual interest and texture to the piece.

Print selection is a little different for dollhouse miniatures, because the size of each patch in a block is so small. One way to help visualize what a print will actually look like in your quilt is to make a window template, which is simply a cutout of an individual patch.

1. Trace a copy of the foundation template for your quilt. Do not include the outer seam allowance.
2. Cut out only the individual patch shape the fabric is intended for.
3. Position the cutout against fabric to see how it will appear in the block. Repeat with additional patches or fabrics if desired.

If the fabric is a medium to large print, chances are the patch will look very different when placed on different areas of the fabric. It doesn't mean you shouldn't use the print, but do be aware that patches won't all look alike unless you take special care to cut and sew each piece in the same manner.

A useful print type for any quilt, including miniatures, is a print that *reads* as a solid. In other words, from a distance it appears to be solid, but on closer inspection you discover a subtle print. These prints introduce texture to a quilt, without adding clutter.

As you build a fabric collection, add fabrics from all color families, even those you don't particularly like. Don't hesitate to use colors together in ways you never imagined. Look at nature, because colors are often combined in ways we don't think of as "matching." Be a good observer, and try to recreate what you see in cloth.

Since dollhouse minis require only small amounts of each fabric, you might consider purchasing assortments of precut six or ten inch squares. They are available from many quilt shops and mail order sources, and are an inexpensive way to add variety to your fabric stash.

Color Value

Stated simply, color value refers to how dark or light a fabric is in relation to others. The amount of contrast between adjoining patches can change the appearance of a block or quilt.

To sort by value

• Pin fabrics you think are of similar value to a wall and stand back. Do any pop out at you as definitely lighter or darker than the others? Remove them from the group and check again.

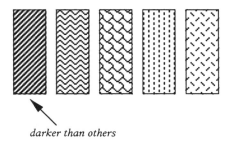

darker than others

• Make black-and-white photocopies of fabric swatches, because color often clouds our judgement. When it is removed, it's easier to judge the true value of a fabric.

• Use a value filter to view fabrics. The filter masks color, giving you a black and white image of fabrics. Take care, most of these filters are red, which makes it difficult to judge red fabrics in relation to others.

If you feel uncertain about fabric selection, browse the library or quilt shops for a book about fabrics and color. There are several written specifically for quilters. Visit quilt exhibits to see how others have combined colors. Most of all, experiment yourself to discover which combinations you like best.

Foundation Piecing Basics

The quilts in this book are all constructed using the same technique many 19th-Century quilters chose, foundation piecing, which totally eliminates the need for exact seams and precisely-cut patches. Even beginners can make a perfect block every time. Foundation piecing opens up a new world of possibilities for miniature crafters who have always wanted to make quilts for their 1-inch scale dollhouses, but felt they just couldn't manipulate all of those tiny bits of fabric.

What is Foundation Piecing?

Patches are sewn to an exact replica of a block, called a *foundation*. For the method used in this book, fabric is positioned on the reverse side of the foundation, with raw edges overlapping drawn lines. When seams are sewn on the front side, directly on the lines, the overlapped edges become seam allowances. If you position fabric correctly, and are careful to sew on the lines, your blocks will be a perfect replica of the foundation. If you don't understand yet, don't worry. Just read through the instructions a few times, then make a few experimental blocks. You'll catch on quickly.

When Can You Foundation Piece?

Foundation Piecing is possible when each new patch covers the entire width of prior patches, such as in the Log Cabin block shown here. Piecing begins at the block's center, and continues outward in a circular motion. Each new log is stitched across the entire length and width of earlier patches.

Sometimes it's not possible to foundation piece a block as one unit, but the accuracy that can be achieved using foundations is good reason to use them for segment piecing. The Twisting Stars block shown below is an example of segment piecing. It is pieced on two foundations, which are sewn together to complete the block. It would have been much more difficult to sew an accurate miniature block using traditional patch-to-patch techniques.

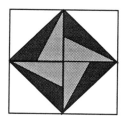
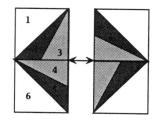

Foundation Materials

Foundations can be temporary or permanent, with each type exactly what its name implies.

•Temporary Foundations

Temporary foundations are removed from blocks before the quilt is sandwiched with batting and backing.

- Vellum or smooth tracing paper is my favorite temporary foundation for quilts of all sizes. It remains stable as blocks are assembled, but when sewing is complete it tears away easily without loosening or distorting the stitches. Seam lines are visible from both sides of the paper, so you can use smaller patches, because you know exactly where to position fabric. When pressed, fabrics stick slightly to this type of paper, which keeps the unit crisp and stable as new patches are added.
- Another choice is plain newsprint. It is easier to remove than heavier bond papers, and is available in pads at most office supply stores.
- Tissue paper is easy to remove, but sometimes tears away before the block is complete.
- Commercial foundation materials are available from mail order sources and quilt shops.

•Permanent Foundations

Permanent foundations remain in the quilt forever.
- Muslin is a commonly used permanent foundation, but I do not recommend it for dollhouse quilts. Muslin foundations sometime stretch out of shape as blocks are assembled, resulting in distorted blocks.
- Nonwoven interfacing is a less bulky, more stable choice for permanent foundations. Used fabric softener sheets (the sheer type) can also be used. Starch and press sheets before marking.

Avoid using heavy permanent foundations for dollhouse quilts that will be placed on a bed. The extra layer makes it harder to hand-quilt, and more difficult to drape the piece on the bed.

The stiffness of permanent foundations might be welcome for some projects, such as blocks that will be used for a miniature wallhanging.

Foundation Accuracy

Foundation templates are block blueprints, and their construction is the one aspect of this method where accuracy is essential. Every line on a foundation becomes a seam line, so if your drawings are not accurate, seams won't be accurate. Accuracy is especially important for dollhouse miniatures, because even small discrepancies are noticeable in tiny blocks.

Narrow lines improve accuracy, because they leave little doubt as to where a seam should be sewn. Ideally, lines should be no wider than the width of the needle as it pierces the foundation. Use a straight edge as a drawing guide, making sure to position it so that traced lines match those on the template exactly.

Transferring Images to Foundations

- If you need just a few foundations, trace each image individually.

•Techniques For Multiple Images

- Trace one or more copies of an image onto a sheet of paper. Stack foundation material with carbon paper, alternating layers. Place the image on top and secure the layers. Use a seamstress's tracing wheel to transfer the image to all layers. Use a straight edge to make sure the wheel rolls directly on marked lines.

- Use a hot iron transfer pen to trace one or more copies of the image onto a sheet of paper, then use the master to heat-transfer foundations onto foundation material. When the image no longer transfers, draw over lines again with the pen, making sure new marks match previous lines. If you use a hot iron pencil, sharpen it often. Avoid pens with wide tips.

- Trace one or more copies of the image onto a sheet of paper. Stack several sheets of foundation paper under the drawing and secure the layers. Sew through lines with an unthreaded needle. Needle holes should form easy-to-follow lines, but should not be so close together that paper falls away during block assembly.

- If you are careful, photocopies can be used. Set the copier to reproduce at exactly 100%. Always copy an original image, because copies of copies are more likely to be distorted. Position the original near the center of the copier's image area, and make sure it is flat. Before using the foundations, compare all copies with the original to verify they are an exact match. If the copier doesn't accept thin papers, select a low-quality, recycled paper, which is usually easier to remove than more expensive bonds.

- Scan templates at 100%. Print images on a laser printer. If you have an ink jet printer, use a dry iron when pressing blocks, otherwise inks could bleed onto fabric. Be especially careful to remove little bits of marked paper that get stuck in seam allowances.

Template Markings

Transfer all numerical markings to foundations. In addition, it is helpful to mark fabric designations on each piece. Since patches are positioned on the reverse side of a drawing, you must always remember that the *finished block will be a mirror image of the printed side of the foundation.* Jotting down a short notation on each area, such as "dark" or "light," is often enough of a reminder to keep the layout accurate as you work.

Grain Placement

To minimize stretchy edges, fabric that lies on the outer perimeter of a block should be cut on the straight grain. Even though we often use odd-sized scraps for the foundation method, it's best if we keep that goal in mind when positioning fabric on the foundations.

If you wish to use a specific print in such a way that a bias edge is on the outside of the block, go ahead and do it, but handle the block carefully during assembly and foundation removal. If you do not wish to worry about grain, consider using a sheer foundation that will remain in the block to permanently stabilize patches.

CHECK POINT
To stabilize stretchy edges, or edges with multiple seam intersections, stitch around the block, approximately $\frac{1}{8}$" from the outer perimeter. Fold the foundation out of the way before sewing.

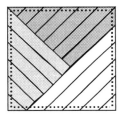

Stitch Length

Fourteen to twenty stitches per inch is usually considered a good stitch length for foundation piecing. For dollhouse quilts, try to stay in the upper range of that guideline, because many blocks contain short seams that tend to pull out easily when longer stitches are used. Stitches should be short enough to remain stable when foundations are pulled away, but not so short that they cause unnecessary wear on the fabric, or are impossible to remove if a seam must be resewn.

The ideal stitch length will vary from project-to-project, depending on the type of foundations and fabric used. For instance, thicker, difficult-to-remove foundations require shorter stitches so that seams remain intact as foundations are pulled away. Longer stitches can be used with permanent foundations. Loosely woven fabrics require shorter stitches to act as a barrier to fraying.

Needle Size

Some quilters prefer to use a needle with a large eye for foundation piecing, because the larger hole it punches makes the foundation easier to remove when the block is complete. I recommend you consider the scale of your quilt when determining needle size. A needle that leaves smaller tracks in the fabric is more appropriate to the delicate scale of a very tiny block.

Trimming Back Seams

It is usually necessary to trim back the seam allowance after sewing each seam. This step removes bulk, and leaves you with a neat, consistent seam allowance. A $\frac{1}{8}$" seam, or just slightly wider, is a good standard for most dollhouse miniatures. Always *trim through all layers*, or your block will end up with a bulky mass of fabric on its reverse side.

Patch Size and Placement

Most recommended patch sizes are based on adding a $\frac{1}{4}$" seam allowance, plus a bit extra to allow flexibility for patch placement. The illustrations are guidelines to help you visualize placement, not absolute rules. Part of the fun of foundation piecing is that you are free to estimate, which speeds up construction. When you are comfortable with foundation piecing, you can probably use smaller patches to assemble blocks. Include a *minimum* of $\frac{1}{8}$" seam allowance on all sides.

Chain Piecing

Block assembly is faster when you chain piece. Read through a few of the patterns to see how pieces are added, then use the following steps to speed up the process. Always make a sample block before cutting all fabric for the quilt.

1. Prepare foundations and cut each one apart slightly past its outermost line.

2. Cut fabric into all required sizes for blocks. Place in stacks near the sewing machine.

3. Add patches 1 and 2 to a foundation. Do not cut threads. Instead, pull the unit slightly and let it hang at the rear of the machine.

4. Pick up the pieces for another block and sew them to a foundation.

5. Continue sewing, adding pieces 1 and 2 to all foundations. Cut strings between blocks, trim back each seam allowance, then press or finger press each piece 2 in place.

6. Add piece 3 to all foundations. Cut apart, trim back, and press. Continue chain piecing remaining patches, adding them in numerical order.

Assembling the Quilt

Sewing Blocks Together

Most quilts are assembled by sewing blocks into rows, then sewing the rows together. In a standard quilt, seam allowances in adjoining rows are pressed in opposite directions before rows are joined. When units are placed right-sides-together for sewing, the opposing lofts butt into each other snugly to help create a perfect match.

Adjoining seams in dollhouse miniatures must often be trimmed back before rows are joined, because their $\frac{1}{4}''$ width creates too much bulk along tiny patches. If trimmed seams are still too bulky, press them open, rather than trimming them more. That method isn't usually recommended for large quilts, because pressing to the side is thought by many to increase seam stability. However, seam strength is of less importance for dollhouse quilts, because they won't be under stress as are nightly-used bed quilts.

Matching-Up Blocks

Some foundation pieced blocks have numerous, bulky seam allowances along their outer edges, which can make it difficult to match intersections when blocks are joined. Stab a straight pin through areas where blocks should meet, such as seam intersections and the points of triangles. Pull pins taut as you sew toward them, to keep fabrics from shifting. Remove the pin to sew through the intersection.

If the pin method doesn't work, take a few hand stitches through points to hold blocks together, making sure the thread passes through the match-points on both foundations. Machine-sew the seam, then check placement and remove the hand stitches.

Removing the Foundations

Remove foundations from seam allowances as you join blocks. Leave remaining foundations in place until borders are added, or for quilts with no borders, until all blocks are sewn together.

Adding Borders

1. For side borders, measure the quilt's length through its vertical midpoint. Never measure at quilt edges, because they are often stretched.

2. Cut two strips to match the measurement in Step 1. To determine width, add $\frac{1}{2}''$ to the desired finished width of the border.

3. Fold a border in half crosswise to determine its midpoint. Pin right-side-down along one side of the quilt, matching midpoints first, then top and bottom edges. Continue matching and pinning the border along the entire length of the side, easing in fullness. If necessary for a good match, remove foundations around the edges of the quilt.

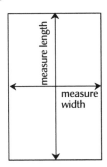

CHECK POINT
Sewing with the fullest side against the feed dogs helps you achieve a pucker-free seam.

4. Use an exact $\frac{1}{4}''$ seam allowance to sew the border to the quilt. Remove papers from the seam. Trim back the seam if you wish, then press open or toward the border.

5. Add a border to the quilt's opposite side.

6. For the top and bottom borders, measure the quilt's width through its horizontal midpoint, including the width of side borders. Cut two borders that length, and the same width as for side borders.

7. Pin a border strip right-side-down along one end of the quilt, matching as for side borders. Ease in fullness if necessary.

8. Use an exact $\frac{1}{4}''$ seam allowance to sew the border to the quilt. Remove papers from seam, trim back, and press.

9. Add the border to the quilt's opposite end in the same manner.

10. Use the same method to add additional borders to the quilt. Remove all foundations from the quilt top.

One of the wonderful aspects of foundation piecing is that to assemble blocks you don't handle tiny, precisely cut pieces, nor must you worry about sewing pieces together with an exact $\frac{1}{4}$" seam allowance.

You do use a $\frac{1}{4}$" seam allowance to join blocks, but if foundation papers are still in place, they create a line to guide you.

Even sewing rows together is a breeze, because when blocks are joined accurately, their outermost seam lines merge into a continuous line exactly $\frac{1}{4}$" from the edge of each row.

After foundation guides are removed, be sure to use a $\frac{1}{4}$" presser foot or marks on the throat plate to gauge an accurate $\frac{1}{4}$" seam.

Design Considerations

Dollhouse miniatures sometimes drape best if blocks are omitted from the bottom corners of the quilt. This allows the sides to fall free, while the bottom edge can be easily tucked between the mattress and footboard. The cutout can be made up entirely of blocks, or by using borders for all or part of the drape.

Miniature beds vary in size, so cutouts may limit the quilt's use to the specific bed it was designed for.

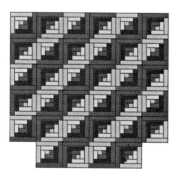

Squaring Up The Quilt

Press the completed quilt top, taking care not to stretch it out of shape. Measure it to make sure it is *square*. In other words, it shouldn't be skewed. The following method may help you square-up the quilt.

• Cut a piece of freezer paper to match the quilt's correct dimensions. Use a permanent marker to draw lines in strategic positions, such as the quilt's center point, row alignment and outer seam allowance.

Press the paper's waxy surface to your ironing board. Use it as a pressing guide, matching areas of the quilt to drawn lines. Stab straight pins through the quilt to hold it in place as you work. Use steam if necessary, but take care to avoid distorting the quilt.

Quilting Designs

If your quilting design must be marked on the quilt, do it now. Avoid rinse-out pens, because some leave images that may come back to haunt you in the future. Mark your quilting designs (lightly) with a very sharp lead, chalk or soapstone pencil.

One option is to quilt *in the ditch*. In other words, along the seam lines (marks aren't necessary).

You may choose to *tie* the quilt. With this method, a single stitch is taken through all layers, then tied with a double knot on the front or back of the quilt. Ties are repeated at regular intervals (see page 12).

Quilt Backing

Use a lightweight fabric for the backing. If you plan to use a self binding, where backing is brought forward and stitched to the quilt front, be sure to choose a fabric that enhances the beauty of the quilt. Cut the backing approximately $1\frac{1}{2}$" wider and longer than the quilt.

Batting

It's sometimes best to eliminate batting in dollhouse quilts, especially ones that contain blocks with many pieces, such as the log cabin. Lots of closely-spaced seam allowances tend to stiffen the quilt, and its ability to drape diminishes with each extra layer. You don't want to spend time making a perfectly-sewn quilt for your dollhouse, and end up with something that resembles a potholder more than it does a bedcover. If you do use batting, try one of the following:

• Silk batting.
• A piece of lightweight muslin or cotton flannel.
• A used sheet of dryer fabric softener (sheer type).

Cut the batting approximately $1\frac{1}{2}$" wider and longer than the quilt

Sandwich the Layers

1. Place pressed backing fabric right-side-down on a flat surface. Hold edges taut with a few pieces of masking tape.
2. If batting is used, center it on top of the backing.
3. Center the quilt right-side-up on the batting. Baste

all layers together with thread, or with small brass safety pins. Take care to avoid wrinkling any layer. Remove masking tape from backing.

Quilting

•Hand Quilting

Quilt as desired using a running stitch. Most quilters use short, sturdy needles called betweens to make the quilting stitch. If you haven't quilted before, purchase a packet that contains multi-sizes to find which best suits your needs.

•Machine Quilting

For machine quilting, you might use a very fine, clear or smoke nylon thread, which gives your quilting stitches depth, but remains nearly invisible in the finished piece. Nylon thread is generally used as the top thread only, not in the bobbin.

•Tying

Tying is an alternative to quilting. Use one or two strands of embroidery floss or other thread. Insert the needle down from the top of the quilt, take a short stitch, then bring it back up from the bottom. Cut the tails about 1" long and tie two square knots. Repeat at intervals across the quilt top. Trim all strands the same length.

Switch direction and knot on the reverse side of quilt if you don't want the threads to show. Cut off threads close to the quilt's surface.

Binding the Quilt

Single fold binding, applied separately to each side, is often the best choice for dollhouse quilts.

1. When you've finished quilting, trim the batting and backing to the same size as the quilt top, squaring up corners a bit if necessary.

2. Measure the quilt vertically as you did for borders. Add one inch to the measurement, then cut two 1" wide strips that length.

3. Place binding right-side-down on the front of the quilt, matching long edges and allowing strip ends to overlap both ends of the quilt. Use a $\frac{1}{4}$" seam allowance to sew the binding to the quilt.

4. Sew the remaining strip to the opposite side of the quilt in the same manner.

5. Trim back each seam allowance to $\frac{1}{8}$", or slightly less. Flip bindings right-side-up. I like to press lightly into the seams from the top side of the quilt.

6. Turn under the raw edge of one binding. Press. Take the folded edge to the back of the quilt. Use matching thread and a blindstitch to sew it to the quilt's backing. Repeat on the opposite side.

CHECK POINT
For a narrower binding edge on the *reverse* side, trim binding width before folding.

7. Cut off excess fabric flush with edges of the quilt.

8. Measure the quilt horizontally as you did for borders. Add two inches to the measurement, then cut two 1" wide strips that length.

9. Sew binding to the top and bottom of the quilt in the same manner as for side binding, centering the strip so that an equal length of binding extends past each end. Trim seam allowance to the same width used for side binding.

10. At each corner, fold tail ends toward the quilt, wrong sides together and flush with the previously bound edges. Trim excess tail length to reduce bulk.

11. Fold under and blindstitch the binding to the quilt.

Option, Bringing the Backing Forward

1. After quilting, trim the batting to match the quilt top, squaring up edges a bit if necessary.

2. Square-up the backing, leaving approximately $\frac{3}{4}$" extending past each edge of the quilt. (You might wish to use a narrower edge.)

3. Fold each side of the backing, wrong sides of fabric together. Bring the folded edges to the front of the quilt. Blindstitch in place.

Draping the Quilt

If the quilt is difficult to drape or tuck-in:
• Dampen the quilt, then mold it to the bed.
• Insert fine gauge, stainless steel wire into seam allowances around the outer edges of the quilt. Bend wires to shape the quilt to the bed.

Quilter's Glossary

appliqué
Sewing small pieces of fabric to a larger background.

backing
The fabric panel used as the back piece of a layered quilt.

backstitch
Stitching backwards over previous stitches to strengthen a seam. In quilting, used most often during setting-in.

basting
Securing two or more fabric layers together with long stitches or safety pins in preparation for final sewing.

batting
The material used as a filler between the quilt top and backing.

bearding
Occurs when batting fibers migrate through the quilt's top or back.

betweens
Short, sturdy needles used for the quilting stitch.

bias
A 45° angle to the fabric's straight grains.

binding
A long, narrow strip of cloth that encases the raw edges of a layered quilt.

bleeding
Occurs when dye is lost from a fabric.

chain piecing
Assembly-line piecing. Units are fed through the machine one after another without breaking threads between them.

concave curve
A curve that rounds inward.

convex curve
A curve that rounds outward.

easing
Adjusting adjoining units of uneven lengths so they match for sewing.

fat eighth
An eighth yard cut of fabric that measures 9" x 22".

fat quarter
A quarter yard cut of fabric that measures 18" x 22".

foundation template
An exact copy of a block or portion of a block. Fabric is sewn directly to the foundation.

loft
The thickness of a batt. Low loft batting is most useful for small quilts.

meander quilting
Random quilting stitches that move across the quilt. They generally do not overlap.

on point
Positioning a block so that it's corners are in a vertical and horizontal arrangement.

patchwork
Small pieces of fabric that are sewn together to form a larger piece. The act of sewing them together is called *piecing*.

pressing
Setting an iron up and down on top of units to press seams and remove wrinkles.

quick piecing
Sewing techniques that eliminate the handling of individual patches.

sashing
Plain or pieced strips that are sewn between blocks.

seam allowance
The width between the seam line and the outer edge of patches. We normally use a $\frac{1}{4}$" seam allowance in quilting.

selvage
The outer, finished edges of fabric that run parallel to the lengthwise grain.

setting
The way elements of a quilt are sewn together.

setting-in
Sewing a patch into an opening created by previously joined patches.

setting square
A plain square of fabric sewn between pieced or appliqué blocks.

setting triangle
A triangle used to fill in the jagged edges left around the outer perimeter of a quilt where blocks are placed on-point.

sharps
Long, thin needles used for appliqué and other hand sewing.

stipple quilting
Closely spaced, random quilting stitches that flatten the quilted area. Often used around appliqué motifs.

straight set
Placing blocks so that their straight sides are parallel to the sides of the quilt.

strip piecing
A quick piecing technique where long strips of fabric are joined into strip sets that mimic a portion of a block. Short segments are cut from the set, then sewn with other segments to form the desired layout.

template
A rigid, exact copy of a pattern piece.

walking foot (or even-feed foot)
A sewing machine presser foot with an advancing mechanism that works with feed dogs to advance both layers of a unit at the same rate.

warp threads
The long threads secured to ends of a loom during the weaving process. They become the lengthwise grain.

weft threads
The threads that are woven across the warp threads. They become the crosswise grain.

Little Sunshine Logs

Although the basic design has been in existence much longer, many quilt historians agree the Log Cabin quilt's upsurge in popularity coincides with Abraham Lincoln's Log Cabin presidential campaign in 1860. Today, the log cabin block remains one of the most popular quilt patterns of all time.

The success of most log cabin quilts, including this example of the Sunshine and Shadows layout, depends on a good amount of contrast between different areas of the block. To make a similar quilt, fabrics in the same side of each block should blend. There should be enough contrast between opposite sides to form a distinct diagonal line in the finished block.

Quilt Size	5¾″ x 7″
Number of Blocks	24
Block Size	1″ square

Materials	Amount
Light Fabrics	⅛ yard
Dark Fabrics	⅛ yard
Backing, Batting & Binding	See Basics Chapter

Cutting	Qty.	Dimensions
Light Fabrics	4	¾″ x 42″ strips*
Dark Fabrics	5	¾″ x 42″ strips*

*or equivalent scraps

Getting Ready

1. Use Template 1A, on page 17, to make 24 piecing foundations. Cut out each foundation slightly past its outermost line.

Making a Block

1. For log 1, cut an approximate ¾″ x ¾″ square from a light strip. The size needn't be exact. Your goal is for the fabric to cover the log, plus provide enough overlap for a stable seam allowance along all sides of it.

2. Position the square right-side-up on the reverse (unprinted) side of the foundation, with the area for log 1 at its center. Use a dab of gluestick to secure the patch. Hold the foundation up to the light, printed side facing you. You should be able to see a shadow of the square. Does it overlap all lines for log 1? Is the overlap enough to create a stable seam allowance (at least ⅛″) when those lines are sewn? If not, reposition and check again.

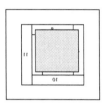

3. Select a dark fabric for log 2. Cut a square from the end of the strip, the same size as for log 1.

4. Position log 2 right-side-down on top of log 1, aligning all edges. Log 2 will completely cover log 1.

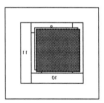

5. Holding fabrics in place, turn the foundation over. Sew directly on the line that separates log 1 from log 2, beginning and ending two or three stitches on either side of the line.

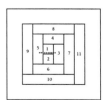

6. Trim the seam allowance if necessary to reduce bulk. Flip log 2 right-side-up. Press or finger-press in place. All unsewn edges of the log should extend past future seam lines by at least ⅛″.

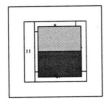

7. Log 3 runs vertically alongside logs 1 and 2. Cut an approximate ⅞″ length from a dark strip. Align the strip right-side-down on top of logs 1 and 2.

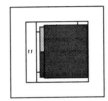

8. Holding fabrics in place, flip the foundation over and sew on the line separating log 3 from logs 1 and 2, beginning and ending two or three stitches on either side of the line.

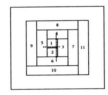

9. Trim the seam allowance if necessary. Flip log 3 into a right-side-up orientation. Press or finger press log in place.

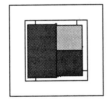

CHECK POINT
Always check patch placement after each log is added. After flipping a log right-side-up, its unsewn edges must extend past future seam lines by at least ⅛″.

10. Add Log 4 in exactly the same manner. Cut an approximate ⅞″ length from a light strip and align it right-side-down, its top edge extending at least ⅛″ above the lines that represent the tops of logs 1 and 3.

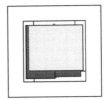

11. Turn to the front side of the foundation and sew on the line that separates log 4 from logs 1 and 3, beginning and ending a few stitches on either side of the line. Trim seam allowance, and flip log 4 into a right-side-up orientation. Press or finger-press log in place.

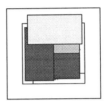

12. Continue adding remaining logs in exactly the same manner, working in numerical order. The foundation will begin to look more like a log cabin block as you add more logs. When you reach the outer four logs, be sure that when flipped right-side-up all unsewn edges stretch past the outer printed line of the foundation.

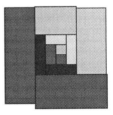

13. Press the block. Use rotary cutting equipment or very sharp scissors to cut through the foundation and fabrics on the outer edge of the outermost printed line. This step creates an exact ¼″ seam allowance around the block's perimeter. Do not remove the foundation.

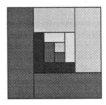

14. Make a total of twenty-four blocks.

Assemble the Quilt Top

1. Arrange blocks in six rows, each containing four blocks.

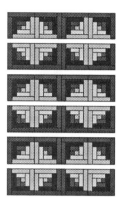

2. Sew blocks in each row together, matching edges carefully. Remove foundations from the seam allowances and trim back. Press seams open or to one side.

3. Pin and sew rows together, matching seam intersections carefully.

4. Remove paper from the new seam allowances and trim back if you wish. Press seams open or to one side.

Make The Pieced Border

Use leftover strips of dark and light fabrics to make a simple pieced border.

1. Use the entire image of Template 1B to make two side border foundations.

2. Use a portion of Template 1B to make a bottom border foundation, as indicated by the shorter arrow. The space between the dotted lines at the left end of the template represents the ending $\frac{1}{4}$″ seam allowance.

3. Cut a patch approximately $1\frac{3}{8}$″ long from a dark or light strip. Place it right-side-up at one end on the reverse side of a side border foundation, making sure its edges overlap the outer lines of the foundation, and the seam line between the first two pieces.

4. Cut another patch from a contrasting strip and place it right-side-down on top of the first. Holding fabrics in place, flip to the front side of the foundation and sew on the line separating the first two pieces, beginning and ending a few stitches on either side of the line.

5. Trim back seam allowance. Flip the patch into a right-side-up position. Press or finger press.

6. Continue adding patches in the same manner until you reach the end of the border. Press the border, then trim through all layers on the outermost line.

7. Construct remaining borders in the same manner.

8. Matching ends and edges carefully, sew each side border to the quilt. Trim back seams and press open or to one side. Add bottom border in the same way.

9. Remove all foundations.

Finishing Up

1. Refer to instructions beginning on page 11 to sandwich, quilt and bind the quilt.

Template 1A

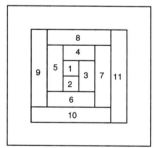

Template 1B   *side borders*

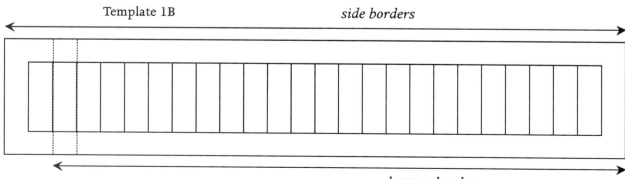

bottom border

Springtime T's

This twin-size T-block quilt goes together quickly and easily. Notice that a mirror image of the T shape emerges when blocks are sewn together, formed by the linking of background pieces. It is most visible when there is good contrast between the T-fabric and the background fabric. Experiment to see the variety of layouts that can be created by simply rotating the orientation of blocks.

Quilt Size	6″ x 8″
Number of Blocks	15
Block Size	1″ x 1″

Materials	Amount
Light Fabric, background	⅛ yard
(2) Dark Fabrics, T shape	5″ x 8″ scrap, each
Dark Fabric, inner border	3″ x 6″ scrap
Light Fabric, middle border	5″ x 7″ scrap
Dark Fabric, outer border	6″ x 10″ scrap
Binding, Backing & Batting	See Basics Chapter

Cutting	Qty.	Dimensions
T Fabric:		
Piece 1	15	1″ x 1¼″
Pieces 5, 6	15	1½″ x 1½″
Background Fabric:		
Pieces 2, 3, 4, 7, 8	38	1⅜″ x 1⅜″
Piece 9	8	1¾″ x 1¾″

Getting Ready

1. Use Template 2A on page 20 to make 15 piecing foundations. Cut out each foundation slightly past its outermost line.

2. Cut each background and T-fabric square reserved for pieces 2, 3, 4, 5, 6, 7, 8 and 9 in half once diagonally.

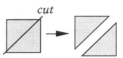

Making a Block

1. Place a 1″ x 1¼″ rectangle right-side-up on the reverse side of a foundation, centering it on top of the area for piece 1.

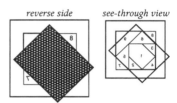

reverse side   *see-through view*

2. Position a piece 2 background triangle right-side-down on top of piece 1, aligning edges.

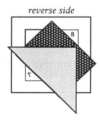

reverse side

3. Holding fabrics in place, turn the foundation over. Sew on the line that separates piece 1 from piece 2, beginning and ending two or three stitches on either side.

4. Trim the seam allowance, leaving at least ⅛″. Flip the triangle right-side-up and finger-press in place. The outer edges of the triangle must extend past the seam lines that define its shape by at least ⅛″.

reverse side

5. Place another 1⅜" background triangle right-side-down along the opposite edge of piece 1.

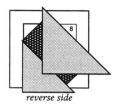

reverse side

6. Holding fabrics in place, flip the foundation over and sew on the line that separates piece 1 from piece 3, beginning and ending two or three stitches on either side.

7. Trim back the seam allowance. Flip the new triangle right-side-up. Press or finger press in place.

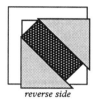

reverse side

CHECK POINT
When flipped right-side-up, patch edges must extend past all lines that will become seam lines for that patch. Patches that lie on the outer perimeter of the block must extend slightly past the outermost line of the foundation.

8. Center a 1⅜" background triangle right-side-down along the lower edge of piece 1.

reverse side

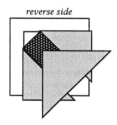

9. Turn over and sew on the line that separates pieces 1 and 4, beginning and ending a few stitches on either side. Trim seam allowance through all layers. Flip triangle right-side-up and finger press in place.

reverse side

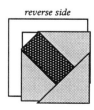

10. Align a piece 5 T-fabric triangle right-side-down on the reverse side of the foundation. Its long edge should overlap the line separating piece 5 from pieces 1 and 2 by at least ⅛". Flip the foundation over and sew on that line, beginning and ending a few stitches on either side.

reverse side

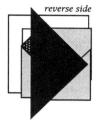

11. Trim the seam allowance through all layers to reduce bulk. Flip the new triangle right-side-up and press or finger press in place.

reverse side

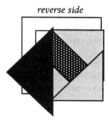

12. Add piece 6 to the opposite side of the block in the same manner. Trim seam allowance and flip upright.

reverse side

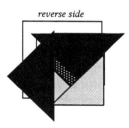

13. For piece 7, align a 1⅜" background triangle right-side-down, its long edge overlapping the line that separates piece 7 from piece 5 by at least ⅛". Flip to the front and sew on that line, beginning and ending a few stitches on either side

14. Trim excess seam allowance from all layers and flip piece upright. Press or finger press in place. Add piece 8 to the opposite side of the block in the same manner. Trim back and flip right-side-up.

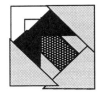

15. Align a 1¾″ background triangle right-side-down near the top of the T. Turn to the front of the foundation and sew on the long line that separates piece 9 from the T triangles.

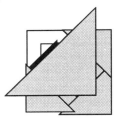

16. Trim excess seam allowance through all layers and flip triangle right-side-up. Press the block.

17. Using rotary cutting equipment or very sharp scissors, cut through the template and fabrics on the outer edge of the outermost printed line.

18. Assemble a total of 15 blocks. Do not remove foundations.

Assemble the Quilt Top
1. Arrange blocks in five rows of three blocks each.

2. Sew rows together with a ¼″ seam allowance, matching block edges carefully. Remove paper from the sewn seam allowances only. Press allowances open or to one side.

3. Pin and sew rows together, matching seam intersections. Be sure to sew on the long printed line created when blocks were joined into rows.

4. Remove paper from the new seam allowances. Press open or to one side.

Add the Borders
1. Refer to the instructions on page 10 to measure and add borders to the quilt. Use ⅝″ wide strips for the inner border, 1″ wide strips for the middle border, and 1¼″ wide strips for the outer border. Adjust widths if necessary to achieve a better fit for your bed.

2. Remove foundations.

Finishing Up
1. Refer to instructions beginning on page 11 to sandwich, quilt and bind the quilt.

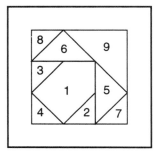

Template 2A

Midnight Stars

This dollhouse quilt is made using only the traditional square-in-a-square block. Eighteen blocks contain light centers, with dark-to-light triangle layers alternating around them. The remaining blocks are the opposite, with medium-dark centers surrounded by light-to-dark triangles. Stars emerge when the blocks are alternated with each other in the layout.

This pattern is suitable for a variety of quilt types: scrappy, Amish, contemporary—or perhaps a layout where each center window features a tiny pictorial print. The choices are yours.

Quilt Size	$5\frac{1}{4}$″ x $7\frac{1}{4}$″
Number of Blocks	35
Block Size	1″ x 1″
Materials	Amount
Dark Fabrics	$\frac{1}{4}$ yard
Light Fabrics	$\frac{1}{4}$ yard
Medium-Dark Fabrics	scraps
Binding, Backing & Batting	See Basics Chapter

Cutting Chart	Qty.	Dimensions & Type
Piece 1	17	$\frac{7}{8}$″ squares, medium-dark
	18	$\frac{7}{8}$″ squares, light
Row 2	34	$1\frac{1}{2}$″ squares, light
	36	$1\frac{1}{2}$″ squares, dark
Row 3	34	$1\frac{5}{8}$″ squares, dark
	36	$1\frac{5}{8}$″ squares, light
Row 4	34	$1\frac{3}{4}$″ squares, light
	36	$1\frac{3}{4}$″ squares, dark

Getting Ready

1. Use Template 3A, on page 23, to make 35 piecing foundations. Cut out each foundation slightly past its outermost line.

2. Cut squares reserved for rows 2, 3 and 4 in half once diagonally.

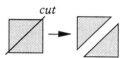

cut

CHECK POINT

If you are making a scrappy quilt, cut $1\frac{3}{4}$″ squares for rows 2,3, and 4. The slightly larger size adds flexibility and speeds-up patch placement, because any piece will fit in any position of the block.

Making a Block

1. Position a $\frac{7}{8}$″ medium-dark square right-side-up on the reverse side of the foundation, centering it on top of the area for piece 1.

reverse of foundation

2. Center a light row 2 triangle right-side-down on top of piece 1.

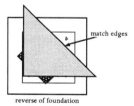

match edges

reverse of foundation

3. Holding fabrics in place, turn the foundation over. Sew on the line that separates piece 1 from the new triangle in row 2, beginning and ending two or three stitches on either side of the line.

4. Trim the seam allowance, leaving at least $\frac{1}{8}$″. Flip the triangle right-side-up. Press or finger-press in place. Be sure all unsewn edges of the triangle extend past the lines that define its shape by at least $\frac{1}{8}$″.

reverse of foundation

5. Add a row 2 triangle to the opposite side of piece 1. Position it right-side-down, aligning and centering its long edge along the lower left edge of piece 1.

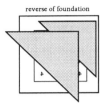

6. Holding fabrics in place, flip the foundation over and sew on the line that separates the new triangle from piece 1, beginning and ending two or three stitches on either side.

7. Trim the seam allowance. Flip the new triangle right-side-up. Press or finger press triangle in place.

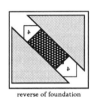

CHECK POINT
As you add triangles, make sure all edges extend past all lines that will become seam lines for that patch.

8. Add the remaining triangles in row 2 in the same manner.

9. Center a dark row 3 triangle right-side-down on the reverse side of the foundation. The long side of the triangle should be centered as closely as possible to the "V" created where two row 2 triangles connect, and should overlap the point of that V by $\frac{1}{8}-\frac{1}{4}''$.

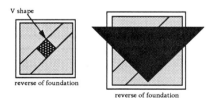

10. Turn the foundation over and sew on the long line separating the new triangle from row 2 triangles, beginning and ending two or three stitches on either side.

11. Trim the seam allowance, cutting away excess fabric from all underlying layers. Flip the new triangle right-side-up. Press or finger-press in place.

12. Add the remaining triangles in row 3, beginning on the side opposite the first as for row 2.

13. Sew light row 4 triangles to the foundation.

14. Press the block. Cut through all layers on the outer edge of the outermost printed line

15. Assemble a total of 17 blocks with this value layout. Do not remove foundations.

16. Assemble 18 blocks with the reverse value layout, each beginning with a light center square and ending with dark triangles around the outer edge.

Assemble the Quilt Top
1. Arrange the blocks in seven rows, each containing five blocks. Alternate block types as shown.

2. Use a ¼″ seam allowance to sew blocks in each row together, matching edges carefully. Remove foundations from the sewn seam allowances only.

3. Press the seam allowances in adjoining rows open or in opposite directions.

4. Pin, then sew rows together with a ¼″ seam allowance. Match seam intersections carefully. Press seams open or to one side.

Finishing Up
1. Refer to instructions beginning on page 11 to sandwich, quilt and bind the quilt.

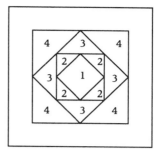

Template 3A

Scrappy Furrows

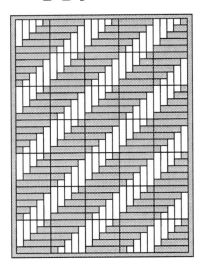

The Half Log Cabin block is foundation pieced in much the same way as the Log Cabin blocks in *Little Sunshine Logs* on page 15. But instead of beginning at the center, piecing starts at the small corner square.

To make a quilt similar to the one shown here, select a scrappy assortment of fabrics. Opposite sides of each block should contrast, but fabrics in same-sides should blend.

Quilt Size	5¼" x 7¼"
Number of Blocks	35
Block Size	1" x 1"

Materials	Amount
Light Fabrics	⅛ yard
Dark Fabrics	⅛ yard
Binding, Backing & Batting	See Basics Chapter

Cutting	Qty.	Dimensions
Light Fabrics	5	¾" x 42" strips*
Dark Fabrics	5	¾" x 42" strips*

*or equivalent scraps

CHECK POINT
Remember that the finished block will be a mirror image of the printed template. To avoid confusion while sewing, mark foundation areas as "light" or "dark."

Getting Ready
1. Use Template 4A, on page 26, to make 35 piecing foundations. Cut out each foundation slightly past its outermost line.

Making a Block
1. Cut an approximate ¾" dark square for log 1. The size needn't be exact. The fabric should cover the log, plus provide enough overlap for a stable seam allowance along all sides.

2. Place the square right-side-up on the reverse side of the foundation, centering it on top of the area for log 1. Secure with a bit of gluestick. Hold the foundation up to the light, printed side facing you. Does the shadow of the square overlap all lines for log 1? Is the overlap enough to create a stable seam allowance when those lines are sewn? The square should also extend slightly past the template's bottom printed edge.

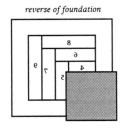

reverse of foundation

3. Select a light fabric for log 2, again cutting a ¾" square. Position the patch right-side-down on top of log 1, aligning all edges.

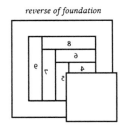

reverse of foundation

4. Hold fabrics in place and turn the foundation over. Sew on the line that separates log 1 from log 2, beginning and ending two or three stitches on either side of the line.

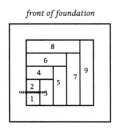

front of foundation

5. Trim the seam allowance to reduce bulk. Flip the light fabric right-side-up, then press or finger-press in place. Be sure the right edge of log 2 extends past the right printed edge of the template.

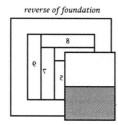

6. For log 3, cut a 1″ length from a dark fabric strip. Align the strip right-side-down, with the left edge of the patch extending at least ⅛″ past the vertical line separating logs 1 and 2 from log 3.

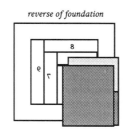

7. Hold fabrics in place, flip the foundation over, and sew on the line , beginning and ending two or three stitches on either side.

8. Trim back the new seam allowance if necessary, then flip log 3 into a right-side-up orientation. Press or finger press log in place.

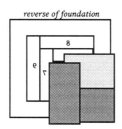

CHECK POINT

After you add a log, make sure unsewn edges extend past all lines that will become seam lines. Since all logs in this block border a portion of the template's edge, the fabric on that edge must extend slightly past the outermost printed line.

9. Log 4 is added in the same manner. Align a 1″ length of light fabric right-side-down, its upper edge extending approximately ¼″ past the horizontal line separating the tops of logs 2 and 3 from log 4.

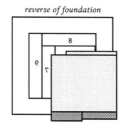

10. Flip to the front side of the foundation and sew on the line, beginning and ending a few stitches on either side. Trim seam allowance, and flip log 4 right-side-up. Press or finger-press log in place.

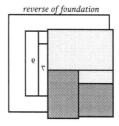

11. Continue adding remaining logs in exactly the same manner, working in numerical order. The chart below lists approximate log lengths.

REMAINING LOG LENGTHS
logs 5 & 6, 1⅛″ each
logs 7 & 8, 1⅜″ each
log 9, 1⅝″

12. Press the block lightly. Cut through all layers on the outer edge of the outermost printed line.

13. Assemble a total of 35 blocks. Do not remove foundations.

Assemble the Quilt Top
1. Arrange blocks in seven rows, each containing five blocks.

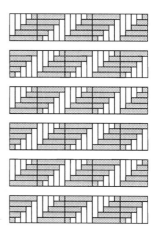

2. Sew the blocks in each row together, matching foundation edges carefully. Remove paper from the sewn seam allowances. Press seam allowances open or to one side.

3. Pin and sew rows together, matching seam intersections carefully as you work. Be sure to sew on the long printed line created when blocks were joined into rows.

4. Remove paper from the new seam allowances. Press open or to one side.

5. Remove all foundations.

Finishing Up

1. Refer to instructions beginning on page 11 to sandwich, quilt and bind the quilt.

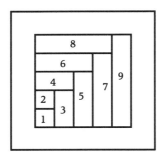

Template 4A

Options

The drawings below illustrate a few more layout options for half log cabin blocks.

Barn Raising Layout

Streak of Lightning Variation

This Way 'N That Way

This dollhouse quilt is assembled by alternating narrow border prints with strips of pieced equilateral triangles. Border prints are fabrics where one or more decorative borders run lengthwise along the yardage. Most are large prints overall, but many contain narrow motifs within the larger pattern that are perfect for dollhouse quilts. Stripes are repeated across the width of the cloth, so yardage requirements are minimal. If you can't find a border print, look for any fabric with narrow, decorative stripes.

Quilt Size	6¾" x 7"
Number Pieced Triangle Strips	5

Materials	Amount
Dark Fabric, for Eq. Triangles	⅛ yard
Light Fabric, for Background	⅛ yard
Border Stripe, finishes at ¾"	16 running inches*
Border Stripe, finishes at ⅝"	32 running inches*
Binding, Backing & Batting	See Basics Chapter

Cutting	Qty.	Dimensions
Dk. Rectangles, Eq. Triangles	90	⅞" x 1¼"
Lt. Rectangles, Background	90	1⅜" x 1⅞"
Narrow Decorative Stripe	3	7¼" long**
Slightly Wider Decorative Stripe	2	7¼" long**

*Allow extra length for matching if you wish stripes to be identical.

**Width depends on stripe.

Getting Ready

1. Use Template 5A, on page 29, to make five piecing foundations. Cut out each foundation slightly past its outermost line.

2. Cut three decorative stripes, each 7¼" long. Cut two slightly wider stripes, each 7¼" long. Stripe width is determined by the individual fabric, but be sure to leave a ¼" seam allowance to the right and left of the design. If you don't use rotary cutting equipment, Template 5B, on page 29, will help you cut stripes. Use graph paper to draft templates of different widths.

3. Cut each background rectangle in half once diagonally to produce two long triangles. Since the triangles within each unit are mirror images of each other, cut half of the rectangles along one diagonal, and the rest along the opposite diagonal.

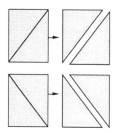

Making an Equilateral Triangle Strip

1. Position a dark rectangle right-side-up on the reverse side of the foundation, centering it over the area for piece 1.

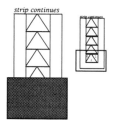

2. Position a light background triangle right-side-down on the dark rectangle.

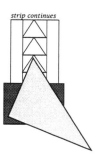

CHECK POINT

Long triangles are a bit trickier to position than symmetrical triangles. The recommended sizes are slightly larger than necessary, to allow you a bit more flexibility for placement. After sewing a triangle, flip it upright and check its position before moving on to the next patch.

3. Holding the fabrics in place, turn the foundation over. Sew on the line that separates pieces 1 and 2, beginning and ending a few stitches on either side.

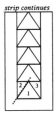

4. Flip piece 2 right-side-up and check its orientation. Its edges must extend past lines that represent future seam lines, and past the outermost line on the right-hand side of the foundation. If alignment is correct, trim the seam allowance and finger press in place.

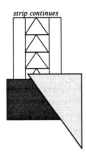

5. Position a mirror image of the first triangle right-side-down on the opposite side of the dark rectangle.

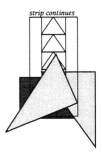

6. Turn the foundation over and sew on the line separating pieces 1 and 3, beginning and ending a few stitches on either side. Check orientation, trim seam allowance, then finger press in place.

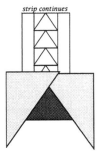

7. Position a dark rectangle right-side-down on the first three pieces, using the finished point of the first equilateral triangle as a placement guide. Match the center of the new rectangle's long edge with the point, overlapping it by at least ⅛″.

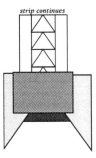

8. Turn the foundation over and sew on the horizontal line that separates the new patch from the first three. Remove from the machine. Trim the seam allowance through all layers and flip the dark patch right-side-up.

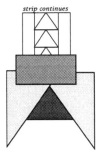

9. Continue adding remaining background triangles and rectangles in the same way. After sewing the final patch, press the unit lightly. Cut on the outermost edge of the foundation to produce a strip of equilateral triangles with a ¼″ seam allowance around its perimeter. Do not remove the foundation.

10. To help keep the long edges of triangles intact, machine-sew a line of stitches approximately $\frac{1}{8}$″ from all edges of the unit. Push the foundation out of the way so that stitches enter only the fabric.

11. Make a total of five equilateral triangle strips.

Assemble the Quilt Top

1. Lay out the pieces of the quilt. Triangle strips are separated by the narrower stripe. The wider stripes become the right and left outer borders of the quilt.

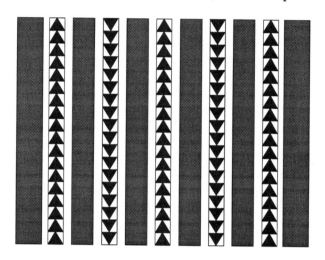

2. Beginning on either side, sew columns together with a $\frac{1}{4}$″ seam allowance. Take care to match the midpoints and ends of each pair as you sew.

3. Trim seams to reduce bulk, then press open or toward the stripes.

4. Remove foundations.

Finishing Up

1. Refer to instructions beginning on page 11 to sandwich, quilt and bind the quilt.

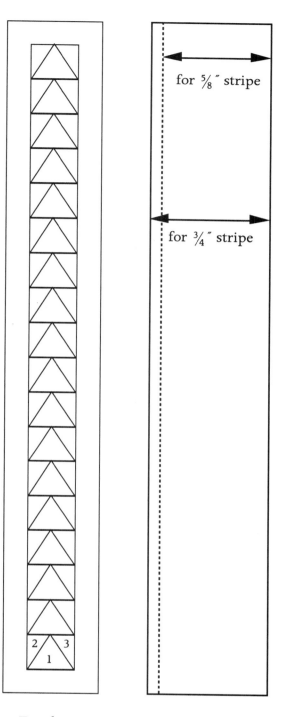

Template 5A   Template 5B

Flying North

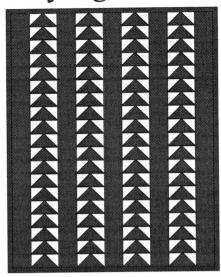

In this quilt, strips of Flying Geese triangles are alternated with a single striped motif cut from a piece of homespun plaid. The stripe finishes at $\frac{1}{2}''$ wide. Make it scrappy, or choose a few vibrant geese fabrics to bring out the colors in your stripe. To widen the quilt, use a wider stripe or additional strips of Flying Geese.

Quilt Size	$5\frac{3}{4}'' \times 7\frac{3}{8}''$
Number of Geese Strips	4

Materials	Amount
Dark Fabric	8" x 13" scrap
Light Fabric	14" x 14" scrap
Plaid Stripe, finishes at $\frac{1}{2}''$	40 running inches
Backing, Batting & Binding	See Basics Chapter

Cutting	Qty.	Dimensions
Dark Squares for Flying Geese	38	$1\frac{1}{2}'' \times 1\frac{1}{2}''$
Light Squares for Background	76	$1\frac{3}{8}'' \times 1\frac{3}{8}''$
Narrow Decorative Stripe	5	$7\frac{5}{8}''$ long*

*Width depends on stripe.

CHECK POINT

When cutting half-square-triangles, we add $\frac{7}{8}''$ to the finished length of a short leg to allow for a standard $\frac{1}{4}''$ seam allowance. The sizes given here are just slightly larger than required, to give you a bit more flexibility for placement. If you find you can consistently align pieces with a $\frac{1}{8}''$ seam, reduce beginning square sizes to $1\frac{1}{4}''$ (geese) and $1\frac{1}{8}''$ (background).

Getting Ready

1. Use Template 6A, on page 32, to make four piecing foundations. Cut out each foundation slightly past its outermost line.

2. Use rotary cutting equipment to cut five stripes, each $7\frac{5}{8}''$ long. Be sure to leave a $\frac{1}{4}''$ seam allowance to the left and right of the design. If you prefer scissors, use Template 6B, on page 32, to cut stripes that finish at $\frac{1}{2}''$ wide. Use graph paper to draft templates for stripes of different widths.

3. Cut each dark square reserved for geese in half once diagonally to produce half-square triangles. Cut each light background square in half once diagonally.

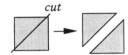

Making a Flying Geese Strip

1. Position a dark geese triangle right-side-up on the reverse side of the foundation, centering it over the area for piece 1.

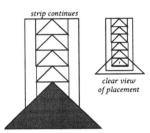

2. Position a light background triangle right-side-down on the dark triangle.

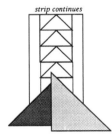

3. Holding fabrics in place, turn the foundation over. Sew on the line that separates pieces 1 and 2, beginning and ending a few stitches on either side.

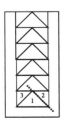

4. Flip piece 2 right-side-up. Check its orientation to make sure unsewn edges extend past all lines that border its shape. The patch should also pass the outermost printed edge of the foundation. If correct, trim seam allowance. Press or finger press triangle in place.

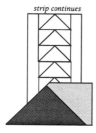

5. Lay piece 3 right-side-down on the opposite side of the dark triangle.

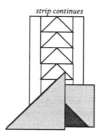

6. Holding fabrics in place, turn the foundation over. Sew on the diagonal line that separates pieces 1 and 3, beginning and ending a few stitches on either side of the line.

7. Flip the triangle right-side-up and verify orientation, then trim the seam allowance. Press or finger press in place.

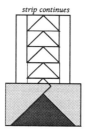

8. Place a dark triangle right-side-down on the first three pieces, using the finished point of the first dark triangle as a placement guide. Center the new triangle's long edge with the point, overlapping it by at least ⅛".

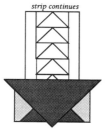

9. Turn the foundation over and sew on the horizontal line that separates the first three patches from the new triangle, beginning and ending a few stitches on either side.

10. Trim-back the seam allowance. Press or finger press in place.

11. Continue adding remaining background and geese triangles in exactly the same way. After sewing the final patch, press the unit lightly. Cut on the outermost edge of the foundation to produce a strip of Flying Geese with a ¼" seam allowance around its perimeter. Do not remove the foundation.

12. Machine-sew a line of stitches approximately ⅛" from all edges of the unit. Push the foundation out of the way so that stitches enter only the fabric. This seam helps keep the edges of background triangles intact.

13. Make a total of four Flying Geese strips.

Assemble the Quilt Top

1. Arrange the columns, beginning and ending with a decorative stripe.

2. Beginning on either side, sew columns together with a ¼″ seam allowance. Take care to match the midpoints and ends of each pair before you sew.

3. Trim seams to reduce bulk, then press open or toward the stripes.

4. Remove foundations.

Finishing Up
1. Refer to instructions beginning on page 11 to sandwich, quilt and bind the quilt.

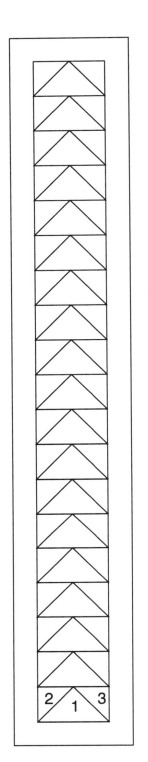

Template 6A

Template 6B

Shoebox Memories

Assembling this dollhouse quilt is a breeze. It's pieced on a single foundation, so it goes together quickly and easily. The example in this book features a pictorial fabric surrounded by 1800's reproduction prints. Don't limit yourself to that theme, because the quilt works well with any type of decor, from vintage to contemporary. It makes a wonderful wallhanging, too.

Traditional yardages are not listed, because this quilt requires only scraps of each fabric used.

Quilt Size		6¼" x 6¼"
Cutting	Qty.	Dimensions
Piece 1, Light	1	2" x 2"
Row 2, Dark	2	1¾" x 1¾"
Row 3, Light	2	2⅛" x 2⅛"
Row 4, Dark	1	1⅛" x 20"
Row 5, Light	2	2¾" x 2¾"
Row 6, Med-Dark	1	1⅜" x 28"
Row 7, Light	1	1⅜" x 18"
Row 8, Dark	2	2¼" x 2¼"

Getting Ready

1. Use Template 7A, on page 35, to make one piecing foundation. Cut out the foundation slightly past its outermost line.

2. Cut each square reserved for rows 2, 3, 5 and 8 in half once diagonally.

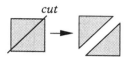

3. Divide each strip reserved for rows 4, 6 and 7 into fourths. An easy way to do this is to fold a strip in half once lengthwise and crease, then fold in half again and crease. Cut apart at creases to form segments.

Making the Quilt

1. Place the 2" x 2" square right-side-up on the reverse side of the foundation, centering it within the lines for piece 1.

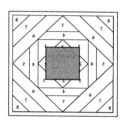

2. Place a row 2 triangle right-side-down on top of the center square, matching and centering its long edge with the edge of the square.

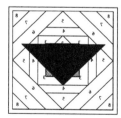

3. Holding fabrics in place, turn the foundation over and sew on the line separating the two pieces, beginning and ending a few stitches on either side.

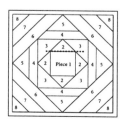

4. Flip the triangle upright and check its orientation. Unsewn edges should extend past all lines that surround its shape. If correct, trim the seam allowance if necessary to reduce bulk, then press or finger press the patch in place.

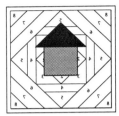

5. Sew a dark triangle to the opposite side of the square in the same way. Repeat to add the remaining triangles to the right and left of the square.

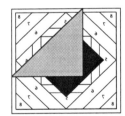

6. Place a row 3 triangle face down, its long edge centered at the corner of the center square, overlapping the corner by approximately $\frac{1}{4}$″.

7. Turn the foundation over and sew on the diagonal line separating the new triangle from row 2, beginning and ending a few stitches on either side. Flip the triangle right-side-up and check orientation. If correct, trim through all layers to create a consistent seam allowance. Finger press patch in place.

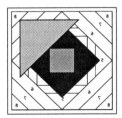

8. Sew a row 3 triangle to the opposite side of the block in the same manner, then add the remaining two triangles in that row.

9. Place a row 4 strip right-side-down on the foundation, centering it at the finished point of a row 2 triangle, and overlapping the point by approximately $\frac{1}{4}$″.

10. Turn the foundation over and sew on the line separating rows 2 and 3 from row 4. Remove from the machine and check to make sure that when flipped right-side-up the strip extends past all lines that surround its shape. Trim seam allowance and finger press in place.

11. Sew a row 4 strip to the opposite side of the block, then add the two remaining strips.

12. Row 5 triangles are aligned by centering their longest edge along row 4 strips, with the edge overlapping the line between rows 4 and 5 by approximately $\frac{1}{4}$″. Sew as for other triangles. When you trim-back seams, be sure to trim through all layers, including the excess tails of straight strips.

13. Add row 6 and 7 strips in the same manner as those in row 4. Add row 8 triangles last. Press the block and trim on the outermost line of the foundation.

14. Remove the foundation carefully to avoid stretching patches. Sew a line of stay-stitches around the outer perimeter of the block, approximately ⅛" from edges.

Finishing Up

1. Refer to the instructions beginning on page 11 to sandwich, quilt and bind the quilt.

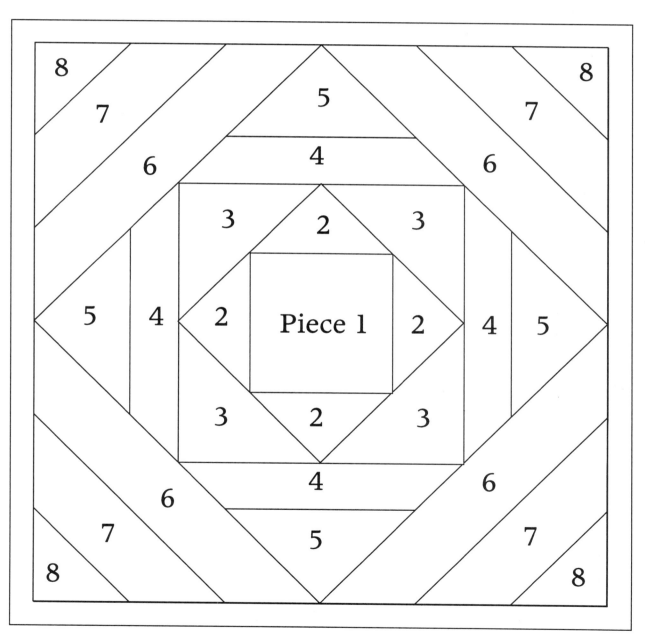

Template 7A

Watercolor Weaves

This variation of the log cabin block is just as versatile as its traditional counterpart. Color value can be arranged in a similar manner as this example, or altered from block to block to add variety. Numerous layout options are possible, and the number increases when you use vellum foundations, which make it easy to see lines from both sides of the paper. Assemble some of the blocks as you normally would, with fabric sewn to the reverse side of foundations. Sew fabric to the front of foundations in remaining blocks, to create mirror images of the first set. Rearrange the blocks until you find a layout you love.

Quilt Size	$4\frac{3}{4}$" x $4\frac{3}{4}$"
Number of Blocks	16
Block Size	$1\frac{1}{8}$" x $1\frac{1}{8}$"

Yardage

Light Fabrics	$\frac{1}{8}$ yard
Medium-Light Fabrics	$\frac{1}{8}$ yard
Medium Fabrics	$\frac{1}{8}$ yard
Backing, Batting & Binding	See Basics Chapter

Cutting	Qty.	Dimensions
Light Fabrics	5	$\frac{5}{8}$" x 42" strips*
Medium-Light Fabrics	4	$\frac{5}{8}$" x 42" strips*
Medium Fabrics	5	$\frac{5}{8}$" x 42" strips*

*or equivalent scraps

Getting Ready

1. Use Template 8A, on page 38, to make 16 piecing foundations. Cut out each foundation slightly past its outermost line.

FABRIC OPTIONS

—Use long strips to add the logs in this quilt, then trim away excess length after sewing each pair of patches together. Or,

—Use shorter lengths of fabric. Allow enough seam allowance at the ends of each log to compensate for diagonal edges.

—If you find it's easy to place patches with an accurate $\frac{1}{8}$" seam allowance, reduce strip width to $\frac{3}{8}$"-$\frac{1}{2}$".

Making a Block

1. Place a medium-light fabric right-side-up on the reverse side of the foundation, centering it on top of the area for piece 1. Patch edges should extend past all future seam lines, and past the outermost printed line on the foundation.

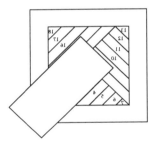

2. Place another medium-light fabric right-side-down on top of the first.

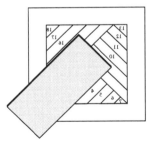

3. Holding fabrics in place, turn the unit over and sew on the line separating pieces 1 and 2, beginning and ending a few stitches on either side.

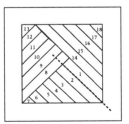

4. Trim-back the seam allowance to approximately 1/8″. Flip piece 2 right-side up. Finger press in place.

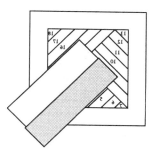

5. Add pieces 3 through 7 in the same manner as piece 2. Before trimming seam allowances, flip each log right-side-up to make sure it extends past all future seam lines. Outer edges should extend slightly past the outermost printed line of the foundation.

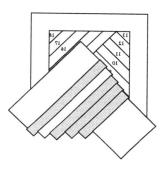

6. Place a light strip right-side-down on top of the first logs. Its upper edge should overlap the line that separates piece 8 from the first set of logs by about 1/4″.

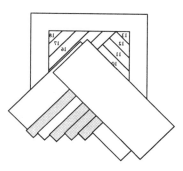

CHECK POINT
If you have difficulty determining where seamlines are, stab a straight pin through the front side of the foundation, directly on the line in question. Note where it passes through the fabric.

7. Turn the foundation over and sew on that line, beginning and ending a few stitches on either side. Remove from the machine and flip piece 8 right-side-up. If orientation is correct, trim-back the seam allowance and finger-press in place.

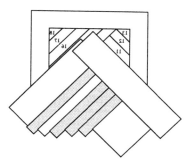

8. Add remaining light logs in the same way.

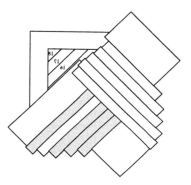

9. The medium logs stretch diagonally across the tops of the earlier logs. Position a medium strip right-side-down on the foundation, making sure its ends extend past both of the printed edges of the foundation.

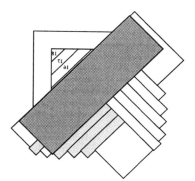

10.   Turn the foundation over and sew on piece 14's longest line, beginning and ending a few stitches on either side. Trim-back the seam if necessary, then flip patch upright. Add remaining medium logs in the same manner. The block may look like a jumbled mess right now, but don't worry, it will shape up after step 11.

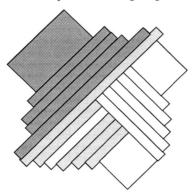

11.   Press the block lightly. Using scissors or rotary cutting equipment, trim the block on the outermost line of the foundation.

12.   To stabilize the stretchy bias edges that surround the block, fold the foundation out of the way and stitch all the way around the perimeter, approximately $\frac{1}{8}$″ from each edge.

13.   Make a total of 16 blocks. Do not remove foundations.

Assemble the Quilt Top

1.   Arrange the blocks in four rows, each row containing four blocks.

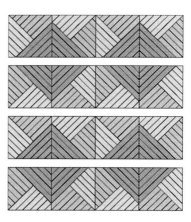

2.   Sew the blocks in each row together. Remove foundations from seam allowances.

3.   Press seams in adjoining rows open or in opposite directions.

4.   Sew rows together, matching seam intersections carefully. Remove all foundations and press the quilt.

Finishing Up

1.   Refer to the instructions beginning on page 11 to sandwich, quilt and bind the quilt.

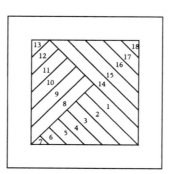

Template 8A

Southwestern Skies

This fabrics in this miniature quilt were chosen from a palette of colors reminiscent of shades seen in the desert southwest. Blocks are straight-sewn in three columns, and columns are separated by single strips of fabric. Adjust quilt width by adding or subtracting columns, or modifying the width of fabric strips. Add more blocks to columns to increase quilt length.

Quilt Size	6½" x 7¾"
Number of Blocks	18
Block Size	1¼" x 1¼"

Yardage

Light Fabric	9" x 16" scrap
Medium-Light Fabric	7" x 14" scrap
Medium Fabric	4" x 7" scrap
Medium-Dark Fabric	5" x 10" scrap
Dark Fabric	10" x 10" scrap
Backing, Batting & Binding	See Basics Chapter

Cutting	Qty.	Dimensions & Type
Piece 1	18	1⅛" x 1⅛" medium
Piece 2	18	1½" x 1½" dark
Piece 3	18	1½" x 1½" med-dk
Piece 4	72	⅞" x 2" light
Piece 5	36	1½" x 1½" med-lt
Column Dividers	4	1⅛" x 8" dark

Getting Ready

1. Use Template 9A, on page 41, to make 18 piecing foundations. Cut out each foundation slightly past its outermost line.

2. Cut squares reserved for pieces 2, 3 and 5 in half once diagonally.

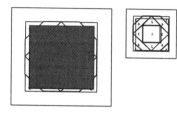

Making a Block

1. Place a 1⅛" medium square right-side-up on the reverse side of the foundation, centering it on the area indicated for piece 1.

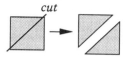

2. Center a dark row 2 triangle right-side-down on the top edge of the medium square.

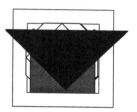

3. Holding fabrics in place, turn the foundation over. Sew on the line that separates the two pieces, beginning and ending a few stitches on either side.

4. Flip piece 2 right-side-up and make sure its unsewn edges extend at least ⅛" past all of its unsewn seam lines. If correct, trim the seam allowance to reduce bulk, then finger press in place.

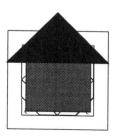

5. Sew a second dark triangle to the opposite side of the square.

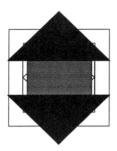

6. Center a medium-dark row 3 triangle right-side-down on the left edge of the medium square.

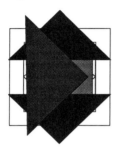

7. Sew triangle to the foundation as you did others, beginning and ending a few stitches on either side of the line that separates the new triangle from the square. Check orientation, then trim seam allowance to reduce bulk. Finger press in place. Add a second medium-dark triangle to the opposite side of the square.

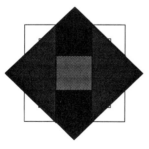

8. Center a light piece 4 rectangle right-side-down along the upper left edge of previous patches.

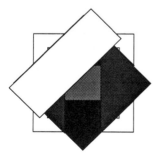

9. Hold fabrics in place and turn the foundation over.

Sew on piece 4's longest diagonal line, beginning and ending a few inches on either side.

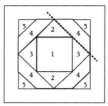

10. Flip the light rectangle right-side-up. Its long edge should extend past the short diagonal line of piece 4, and its tails should overlap the outer lines of the foundation. If correct, trim-back seam allowance and finger press in place.

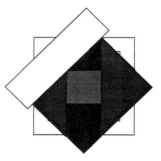

11. Sew a second light rectangle to the opposite edge of the block in the same manner, then add the remaining two rectangles.

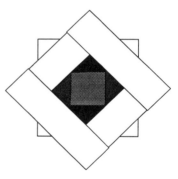

12. The triangles in row 5 are sewn to the block in the same way as previous triangles. Center a medium-light triangle's long edge along the edge of a light rectangle.

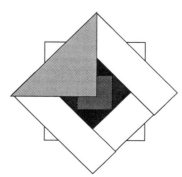

13. Turn the foundation over and sew on the line separating rows 4 and 5. Check Orientation, trim seam, then finger press in place.

14. Sew a medium-light triangle to the opposite edge of the block in the same way, then add the remaining two triangles to complete the block.

15. Press the block. Use scissors or rotary cutting equipment to trim the block on the outermost line of the foundation. Do not remove foundation.

16. Make a total of 18 blocks.

Assemble the Quilt Top

1. Arrange the blocks in three vertical columns, each column containing six blocks. Place a 1⅛″ x 8″ dark strip between each column, and to the left and right of the quilt.

2. Sew blocks in each column together, matching foundation edges carefully. Remove foundations from seam allowances, then press seams open or to one side.

3. Matching midpoints and ends exactly, use a ¼″ seam allowance to sew the dark strips to the columns of blocks. Remove foundations. Trim new seams if necessary to reduce bulk. Press the quilt.

Finishing Up

1. Refer to instructions beginning on page 11 to sandwich, quilt and bind the quilt.

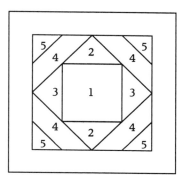

Template 9A

Braided Sunshine

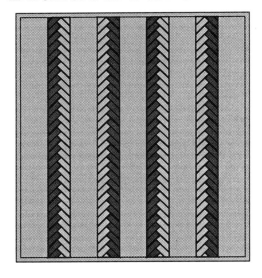

The braided columns in this light and airy little quilt are separated by strips of a fabric that blends with the scrappy assortment of prints used for the light portion of the braids. If you'd like to experiment, eliminate the fabric strips, then sew several pieced columns together side-by-side.

Quilt Size	$6\frac{1}{2}$" x $7\frac{1}{8}$"
Number of Braided Columns	4

Materials

Light Fabrics	$\frac{1}{8}$ yard
Medium-Dark Fabrics	$\frac{1}{8}$ yard
Backing, Batting & Binding	See Basics Chapter

Cutting	Qty.	Dimensions
Light Strips	4	$\frac{3}{4}$" x 42"*
Medium-Dark Strips	4	$\frac{3}{4}$" x 42"*
Light Divider Strips	5	$1\frac{1}{4}$" x $7\frac{3}{8}$"

*or equivalent scraps

Getting Ready

1. Use Template 10A, on page 44, to make four piecing foundations. Because the patches are so tiny, numbers aren't used to indicate the piecing order. The first patch is marked with a tiny ✪. Place a mark in the patch to help you remember where piecing begins. Cut out each foundation slightly past its outermost line.

2. If you plan to chain piece to speed up assembly (page 9), cut each $\frac{3}{4}$" x 42" strip into $1\frac{1}{4}$" long segments. Otherwise, piece with long strips, then trim-back excess tails as you work.

CHECK POINT
If you find you consistently align and sew patches with a $\frac{1}{8}$" seam allowance, $\frac{3}{8}$"–$\frac{1}{2}$" wide strips can be used to piece the braids. This pattern is a great way to use those small scraps you've been saving.

Making a Braided Column

1. Position a light strip right-side-up on the reverse side of the foundation, centering it over the beginning patch. Its edges should overlap all seam lines for the patch, and its lower right edge should extend slightly past the foundation's outermost line.

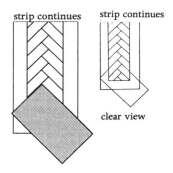

2. Align a medium-dark strip on top of the first, right-side-down.

3.   Holding fabrics in place, turn the foundation over. Sew on the line that separates the first two pieces, beginning and ending a few stitches on either side of the line. Use short stitches for this short seam, to avoid pulling it out when foundations are removed.

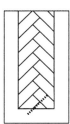

4.   Remove from the machine. Trim-back the seam allowance, then flip the dark strip right-side-up. Its edges should extend past all lines that define its shape, and past the outermost line on the right edge of the foundation.

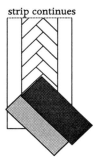

5.   The next patch lies along the top, angled edges of the first two patches. Align a light rectangle right-side-down on the foundation, matching its top edge with the short edges of the first patches, and its right-hand edge with the long edge of the dark patch.

6.   Holding fabrics in place, flip the unit over. Sew on the line that separates the first two patches from the third, beginning and ending the seam a few stitches on either side.

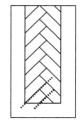

7.   Remove from the machine and turn the foundation over. Flip the new light patch right-side-up and check its orientation. All edges should extend past lines that define its shape, and its lower left edge should pass the outermost line of the foundation.

8.   Sew another medium-dark patch to the opposite side of the braid in the same manner. Flip right-side-up to check orientation. If correct, trim the seam allowance and finger-press in place.

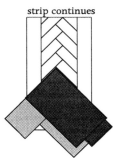

9. Continue adding braids to the strip, moving from side to side and alternating color value.

10. After the last segment is sewn, press the strip lightly. Cut through all layers on the foundation's outer line. Do not remove the foundation.

11. Assemble a total of four pieced braids.

Assemble the Quilt

1. Arrange the columns, beginning and ending with a divider strip.

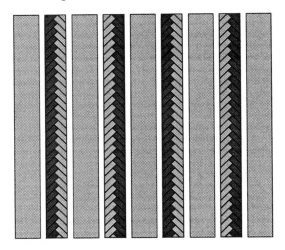

2. Beginning on either side, sew columns together with a $\frac{1}{4}$" seam allowance. Take care to match the mid-points and ends of each pair before you sew.

3. Trim seams to reduce bulk, then press open or toward the dividers.

4. Remove foundations.

Finishing Up

1. Refer to instructions beginning on page 11 to sandwich, quilt and bind the quilt.

Begin here

Template 10A

Quilter's Coloring Book

Little Sunshine Logs, page 15

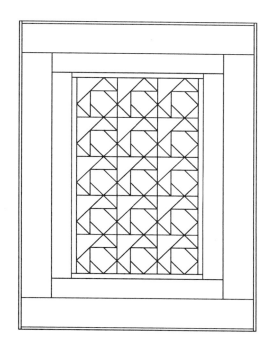

Springtime T's, page 18

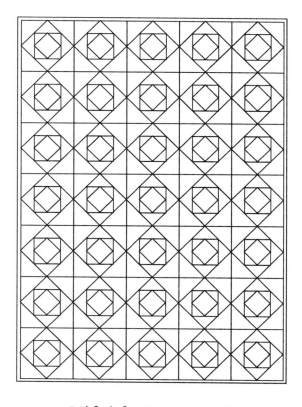

Midnight Stars, page 21

Scrappy Furrows, page 24

Quilter's Coloring Book

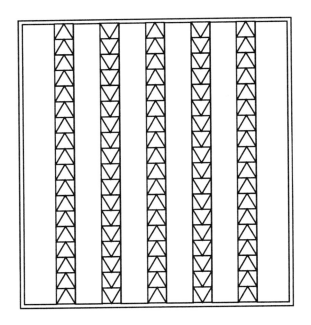

This Way 'N That Way, page 27

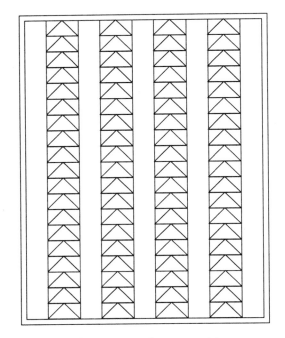

Flying North, Page 30

Shoebox Memories, page 33

Quilter's Coloring Book

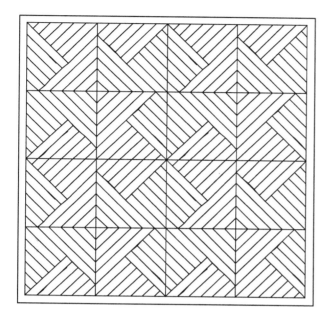

Watercolor Weaves, page 36

Southwestern Skies, page 39

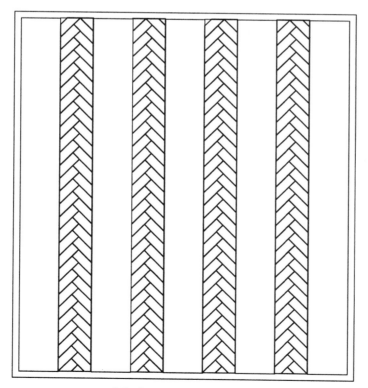

Braided Sunshine, page 42

Quilter's Resources

Mail-Order Sources
for Fabric & Quilting Supplies

Clotilde, Inc.
B3000
Louisiana, MO 63353-3000
books, notions, tools & more
http://www.clotilde.com/

Keepsake Quilting
Post Office Box 1618
Centre Harbor, NH 03226-1618
full range of quilting supplies
http://www.keepsakequilting.com/

Nancy's Notions
Post Office Box 683
Beaver Dam, WI 53916
books, notions, tools & more
http://www.nancysnotions.com/Home.html

Quilts & Other Comforts
Post Office Box 4100
Golden, CO 80401-0100
full range of quilting supplies

Quilting Traditions
Post Office Box 488
Cedar Mountain, NC 28718
silk batting, printed & plain foundations
http://www.UserHome.com/quilting/quilts.html

The Thread Shed
Post Office Box 898
Horse Shoe, NC 28742-0898
wide variety of cotton & specialty threads

Seminar for Miniature Quilt Enthusiasts
MINIATUREFEST
Quilting Traditions
Post Office Box 488
Cedar Mountain, NC 28718
annual seminar especially for
miniature quilt enthusiasts
send long SASE